Weird Butterflies & Moths

Text by RONALD ORENSTEIN

Photography by THOMAS MARENT

FIREFLY BOOKS

A FIREFLY BOOK

Published by Firefly Books Ltd. 2016

First printing

Publisher Cataloging-in-Publication Data (U.S.)
Names: Orenstein, Ronald I. (Ronald Isaac), 1946-, author. | Marent, Thomas, photographer.
Title: Weird butterflies & moths / text by Ronald Orenstein ; photography by Thomas Marent.
Description: Richmond Hill, Ontario, Canada : Firefly Books, 2016. | Includes index | Summary: "High definition images reveal the minute details of rare and fascinating butterflies and moths. The pictures are accompanied with brief descriptions that show just how weird these insects are" – Provided by publisher.
Identifiers: ISBN 978-1-77085-814-5 (paperback) | 978-1-77085-815-2 (hardcover)
Subjects: Butterflies – Pictorial works -- Juvenile literature. | Moths – Pictorial works -- Juvenile literature.
Classification: LCC QL544.2O746 |DDC 595.78 – dc23

Library and Archives Canada Cataloguing in Publication
A CIP record for this title is available from Library and Archives Canada

Published in the United States by
Firefly Books (U.S.) Inc.
P.O. Box 1338, Ellicott Station
Buffalo, New York 14205

Published in Canada by
Firefly Books Ltd.
50 Staples Avenue, Unit 1
Richmond Hill, Ontario L4B 0A7

For my family and especially my mother, Mary Orenstein, who loves butterflies.
—Ronald Orenstein

For my parents, Rose and Richard Marent.
—Thomas Marent

IMAGE CREDITS

All photos copyright © 2016 Thomas Marent except the following:

National Picture Library
Page 63 © Thomas Lazar / naturepl.com

Printed in China

The publisher gratefully acknowledges the financial support for our publishing program by the Government of Canada through the Canada Book Fund as administered by the Department of Canadian Heritage.

INTRODUCTION

I love butterflies. I suspect you do too. To the Blackfeet, butterflies are bringers of dreams. In China they are symbols of long life, beauty and elegance.

This book is about butterflies and moths. Did you know that butterflies are a kind of moth? Moths can be weirder than any butterfly. There are blood-sucking moths, moths with jaws instead of tongues, and moths with no mouthparts at all. There are tiny moths, giant moths and moths with no wings. There are moths that make high-pitched sounds to jam the sonar signals of hungry bats. There are moths that look like bees or wasps, and moths that look like bird droppings.

Of the 200,000 species of moths, only about 17,500 are butterflies. Butterflies have been visiting flowers and drinking their nectar for 100 million years—almost as long as there have been flowering plants. But moths have been around for far longer, perhaps 230 million years.

Moths (including butterflies) are insects. They have six legs. Adults have two pairs of wings, called forewings and hindwings. Tiny colored scales cover these wings. That's why scientists call them Lepidoptera, which means "scaly wings." Most moths (and butterflies) drink through a coiled "tongue," or proboscis. They have huge compound eyes and a pair of antennae. The antennae can help you tell butterflies from other moths—butterfly antennae are tipped with little knobs.

Some butterflies fly very long distances (the US Air Force wants to develop tiny robots that fly the way butterflies do). Migrating Monarch butterflies find their way south and then north again by following the sun's position in the sky. They use "sun compasses" in their brains and "clocks" in their antennae. On cloudy days they probably use another type of compass—one that tracks the earth's magnetic field.

Butterflies and moths go through four life stages: egg, caterpillar, pupa and adult. Most caterpillars eat leaves, but some eat flowers and others are carnivores. Caterpillars of Britain's smallest butterfly, the Small Blue, will eat flowers, growing seeds, and other caterpillars.

Monarch butterfly caterpillars eat milkweed and store the plant's poisons in their own systems. Predators stay away from Monarchs! Another butterfly, the Viceroy, looks like a Monarch, so predators may stay away from Viceroys too. Butterflies that copy other insects are called mimics. D'Almeida's Glasswing (pp 14–15) is one of about 200 butterflies in tropical America that copy each other.

Butterflies and moths are losing their homes to farming, logging, mining and city-building. Pesticides kill them. Weed killers destroy the plants they need to survive. Climate change is a growing problem. Butterflies and moths need your help!

You can turn your yard into a butterfly garden, full of plants that butterflies like to visit. Check out http://climatekids.nasa.gov/butterfly-garden/ to find out how. Monarch Watch sells seed kits for growing milkweed and nectar plants. You can use them to create a "way station" for migrating Monarchs in your yard or at school (http://www.monarchwatch.org/waystations/seed_kit.html).

In England you can join a moth count to help record more than 900 species (http://www.mothscount.org/). You will find more ideas and information at the Children's Butterfly Site (http://www.kidsbutterfly.org/).

If you love butterflies (and moths), there is a lot you can do!

4

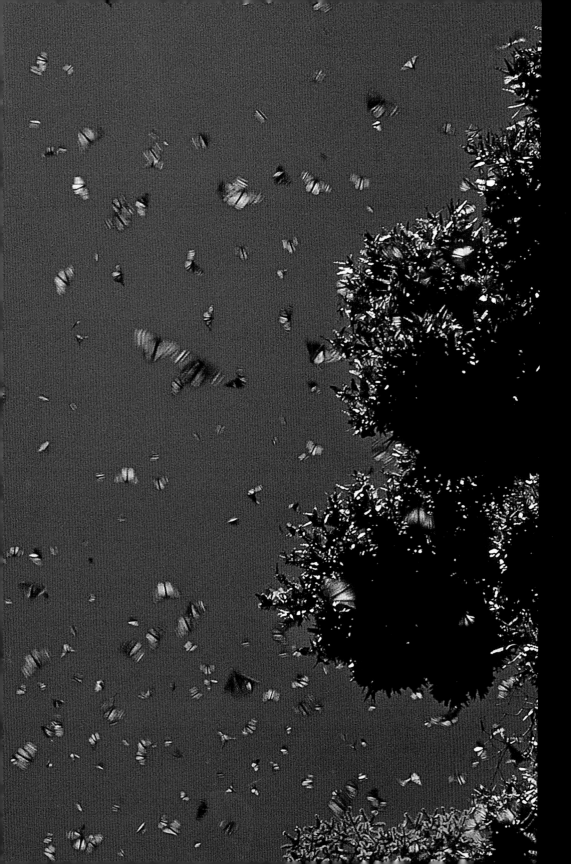

MONARCH

Danaus plexippus

Every year, millions of Monarch butterflies fly south to Mexico and California. These eastern Monarchs are spending the winter in the pine forests of the Monarch Butterfly Biosphere Reserve in Michoacan, Mexico. Sadly, illegal loggers have cut down almost half of these forests. In the USA and Canada, spraying farmland with weed-killing chemicals has destroyed many milkweed plants. But Monarch caterpillars need milkweed for food. Today there are far fewer Monarchs than just a few years ago.

COMMON MORPHO

Morpho helenor

The wings of most butterflies and moths are covered with tiny scales, which overlap like shingles on a roof. Scales give the wings their colors and patterns. Some wing colors help a butterfly to hide, and others help male butterflies show off to the females. Many butterflies have spots on their wings that look like eyes. Small birds are frightened by large, staring eyes. Eyespots, like the ones under the wing of this Common Morpho from South America, may help scare them away.

11

FOREST GIANT OWL

Caligo eurilochus

The Forest Giant Owl is a large butterfly from South America. The eyespots on its wings have a white "sparkle" in the center. This sparkle looks like the highlight in a real eye—perhaps the eye of an owl or a snake. And it may look even bigger to a hungry bird. This is because the sparkle reflects ultraviolet light. We can't see ultraviolet light, but birds can, so to them the sparkle looks much bigger. Scientists found that birds were afraid of a model butterfly with eyespots. They were even more frightened if the eyespots had sparkles in them.

PINK-TIPPED GLASSWING SATYR

Cithaerias pireta

Pink-tipped Glasswing Satyrs live in tropical America. Their wings have lost almost all of their scales. But they still have eyespots, which are made of colored scales. The dark bars on their wings are not made of scales. They are marked directly on the wing itself.

D'ALMEIDA'S GLASSWING

Ithomia arduinna arduinna
Not all butterflies and moths have scales covering their wings. Parts of the wings of these d'Almeida's Glasswings have no scales at all. Glasswings live in the rainforests of tropical America. Their transparent wings can make them hard to see in the dim forest light. This is a mating pair. The male, on the left, has a dark blister on his hindwing. This blister contains special hairlike scales called androconia. The androconia produce chemicals called pheromones, which males release into the air to attract females.

15

Helicopis cupido

Many butterflies have long "tails" on their wings. Tails may help attract a mate. They may also fool a bird into attacking the wrong end of the butterfly. If a bird bites at the tails, it may only get a mouthful of wing— the rest of the butterfly can still escape. The Spangled Cupid lives in the rainforests of northern South America. Groups of more than 20 cupid caterpillars may live together inside one large rolled-up leaf.

SPANISH MOON MOTH

Graellsia isabellae

The Spanish Moon Moth lives in pine forests in the mountains of Spain, France and Switzerland. These moths fly at night, in the dark. Their long tails may help them escape from bats. Many bats make sounds too high for us to hear. They find their prey by following the echoes of their squeaks. When the echoes bounce off the tails of the Luna Moth of North America (a cousin of the Spanish Moon Moth), the bats get confused about where it is. This gives the moth a chance to get away.

17

COMET MOTH

Argema mittrei

The Comet Moth comes from the island of Madagascar. This is a male, and his wing tails may be 6 inches (15 cm) long. Females' tails are broader and shorter. Comet Moths are hard to find in the wild, so moth farmers in Madagascar raise them in captivity. The farmers sell the moths to collectors, and they also sell the silk that the moths spin to make their cocoons. Comet Moth cocoons are full of holes. It is very rainy where they live, and the holes let water drain out so the pupa inside won't drown.

DIRPHIA MOTH

Dirphia species

The bodies of many moths are thickly covered with hairs to keep them warm in the cool night air. Moths don't have knobs at the ends of their antennae the way butterflies do. Instead, many moth antennae look like feathers. The branches on the antennae help the moths pick up chemical signals in the air. These signals may lead them to a mate, to a food plant, or to a place to lay their eggs. This moth comes from the cloud forests of Ecuador.

Unidentified

Many butterflies use bright colors to attract a mate, but colors are no use at night. Night-flying moths, like these from Ecuador, attract mates with chemicals. Many female moths "call" to males by giving off chemicals called pheromones. The males can pick up these chemical calls from a long way off. Some collect bits of pheromone on their huge, feathery antennae. Then they follow the chemical trail to where the female is waiting.

ATLAS MOTH

Attacus atlas

The Atlas Moth comes from China and Southeast Asia. It is one of the world's largest moths. Male Atlas Moths like this one have huge, feathery antennae (the antennae of females are much smaller). The males use their antennae to pick up chemical signals from females as far as 20 miles (32 km) away. They need antennae that work this well, because they must find a mate before they starve to death. Adult Atlas Moths cannot eat, and they live for only about two weeks.

LAPPET

Gastropacha quercifolia

If a predator can't find you, it can't eat you. Moths are very good at hiding from hungry predators. Some use camouflage to blend into the background. Others are masters of disguise—they may look like twigs, leaves or bird droppings. The Lappet, a moth from Europe and Asia, is an expert at camouflage. When it sits on the ground with its wings folded, it looks like a clump of dead oak leaves.

VARIABLE CRACKER

Hamadryas feronia

The Variable Cracker of tropical America depends on camouflage. Crackers perch head down on tree trunks. If they pick the right tree, they blend in with the bark. Crackers change color as they get older. Naturally, they prefer backgrounds that match their color. Sometimes a male will perch on white bark, where he is easy to see. He may be trying to show off to females. If a female or a rival male flies by, he will chase it. As he flies, special veins in his wings make loud snapping sounds. This is why these butterflies are called "crackers."

SILKY OWL

Taenaris catops

The Silky Owl lives in the rainforests of New Guinea. It is a large butterfly, almost 4 inches (10 cm) across, with rounded hindwings and large eyespots. Silky Owls fly in the lower levels of the forest. They feed on the juices of ancient palm-like plants called cycads. Cycad juices are rich in poisons, which the butterflies store in their own bodies. Their coloring may be a warning that they are not safe to eat.

WHITE-ANGLED SULPHUR

Anteos clorinde
A flying White-angled Sulphur is easy to see. The upper sides of its wings are white, with a bright yellow patch on each forewing. The patches may look even brighter to another butterfly than they do to us. They reflect ultraviolet light, which butterflies can see but we can't. When this butterfly lands and folds its wings, it is much harder to spot. This is because the shape of its wings and the coloring underneath them make the butterfly look like a green leaf. White-angled Sulphurs are found from southern Texas to Argentina.

AFRICAN TIGER MOTH

Alytarchia leonina
Some butterflies and moths roost together in large numbers. This is a group of tiger moths in Tanzania's Gombe Stream National Park, where Jane Goodall studied wild chimpanzees. Their bright colors warn hungry predators that their bodies are filled with poisonous chemicals. If an enemy attacks them anyway, the moths fly up in a fluttering cloud of wings. That may be enough to startle the predator and give the moths a chance to escape.

NARROW-BORDERED BEE HAWKMOTH

Hemaris tityus

Some day-flying moths look and act like bees and wasps. The Narrow-bordered Bee Hawkmoth looks like a bumblebee. It flies like one too. Other day-flying moths look like wasps or hornets. Moths can't sting. But if they look and act like an insect that can sting, they may fool birds and other hungry predators. If their enemies think they can sting too, they may stay out of their way.

HUMMINGBIRD HAWKMOTH

Macroglossum stellatarum

The Hummingbird Hawkmoth visits flowers by day.
It hovers in front of them, beating its wings very quickly.
Then it stretches out its long tongue to drink their nectar.
People often mistake Hummingbird Hawkmoths for real
hummingbirds. But these moths are
not copying hummingbirds—they live in Europe
and Asia, where there are no hummingbirds. They
just happen to look alike, because hawkmoths and
hummingbirds feed in the same way.

HAMADRYAD

Tellervo zoilus

The Hamadryad is a black and white butterfly with orange eyes. It is common in the tropical rainforests of Queensland, Australia. Hamadryads fly slowly through the lower parts of the forest. The males gather in sunny spots to show off for females. The Hamadryad is a cousin of the Monarch butterfly, and like the Monarch, it is bad-tasting. Some other Australian butterflies look and act like a Hamadryad, even though they are not close relatives. Instead, they are mimics. By pretending to be evil-tasting Hamadryads, they may fool predators into leaving them alone.

HEWITSON'S PINK FORESTER

Euphaedra hewitsoni

Many tropical butterflies never visit flowers. Instead, they feed on rotting fruits. Foresters are African butterflies that search eagerly for fallen figs and other fruits. These foods give butterflies both sugar and protein, while flowers usually provide only sugar. The protein helps adult foresters live longer than butterflies that visit only flowers—up to 10 months. This protein may also help the females to produce more eggs.

DARWIN'S MOTH

Xanthopan morgani praedicta

In 1862 the famous naturalist Charles Darwin received a strange orchid from Madagascar. It carried its nectar at the bottom of a tube almost a foot (30 cm) long. Darwin wrote to a friend, "Good heavens, what insect can suck it?" He guessed that there must be a moth in Madagascar with a foot-long tongue. In 1903, 20 years after he died, scientists discovered and named Darwin's Moth. It does have a foot-long tongue—Darwin was proved right.

PUDDLING BUTTERFLIES IN THAILAND

Left to right: Straight Pierrot (*Caleta roxus*); Zebra Blue (*Leptotes plinius*); several Common Gulls (*Cepora nerissa dapha*); Tree Yellow (*Gandaca harina*); Jay (*Graphium species*); Orange Emigrant (*Catopsila scylla*); Common Grass Yellow (*Eurema hecabe*). Many butterflies land on damp ground to get mineral salts. This is called puddling. In tropical forests, many kinds of butterflies may puddle together. For instance, in Thailand you might find 30 or 40 species in a single group. Puddling butterflies are almost always males. They use some of the salt themselves, and the rest they give as a "gift" to females when they mate.

88 BUTTERFLY AND HUMBOLDT'S PERISAMA

Diaethria marchalii and *Perisama humboldtii*
These puddling butterflies were photographed in Peru.
Eighty-eight butterflies get their name from markings
on the underside of their wings. The males are regular
puddlers. They spend the morning high in the forest
canopy, then in the afternoon they fly down to the
ground to drink. Eighty-eights will drink from soil,
stones, road surfaces and walls. They will even drink
sweat from human skin.

THICK-EDGED KITE-SWALLOWTAIL

Eurytides orabilis

When rainforest butterflies drink, they may not be thirsty for water. They need salt, and they may have to drink a lot of water to get the salt they need. But they don't need the extra water, so they get rid of it while they are drinking. This butterfly from Colombia is drinking and spraying out a jet of extra water at the same time.

MOUNTAIN GREEN-VEINED WHITE

Pieris bryoniae

Butterfly eggs come in many shapes and sizes.
The Mountain Green-veined White lays eggs like little
barrels, marked with grooves that run from top to
bottom. The eggs may be orange or pink. The color
may warn other female butterflies to lay their eggs someplace
else—this spot has already been taken! Mountain Green-veined
Whites live in the mountains of Europe and Asia.

MAP

Araschnia levana

The Map is a butterfly from Europe and Asia. Nettles are the only plants that its caterpillars eat. A female Map lays her eggs in long chains, which she hangs from the underside of nettle leaves. The Map's egg chains look like nettle flowers, which are very small and grow in long clusters. Does this fool predators looking for butterfly eggs? No one really knows.

41

GIANT PEACOCK MOTH

Saturnia pyri
No insect has more than six legs, and some caterpillars don't have any. The "legs" of this Giant Peacock Moth caterpillar are really false legs—called prolegs—which are tipped with tiny claws. The claws help the caterpillar hold on to stems or leaves. Prolegs do not work like real legs. As it moves, the caterpillar pumps liquid into its prolegs, which makes them swell up. They get larger until their hooks can grab the surface that the caterpillar wants to walk over.

GIANT PEACOCK MOTH

Saturnia pyri
The Giant Peacock Moth is the largest moth in Europe. When its caterpillars are full-grown, they are covered with sky-blue bumps called scoli. Hollow black bristles grow out of the scoli. If the caterpillar is disturbed, the bristles give off a mixture of poisonous chemicals, which may drive away attacking ants or birds. Threatened Peacock Moth caterpillars make high-pitched chirping sounds by scraping their jaws together. These chirps may warn predators that the caterpillars are armed with chemical weapons.

VARIABLE CRACKER

Hamadryas feronia

If you disturb a cracker caterpillar, it strikes out with the spiky horns behind its head.

ALDER MOTH

Acronicta alni

CHINESE MOON MOTH

Actias dubernardi
Most moth caterpillars use camouflage to hide
from their enemies. Chinese Moon Moth caterpillars feed on
pine needles. Fully-grown caterpillars have white or silver lines on
their bodies. These lines seem to break up their shape so that a bird might mistake
the caterpillar for a cluster of pine needles. The caterpillars take about
six weeks to grow, and then they spin a cocoon. Inside the cocoon, the pupa may
take a few months to become an adult. The adult Chinese Moon Moth is pink and
pale green, with very long tails on its wings. It lives for only a few days.

48

ORANGE-SPOTTED TIGER CLEARWING

Mechanitis polymnia
Orange-spotted Tiger Clearwings live in tropical America. Their caterpillars are hunted by ants. They have an odd way of defending themselves. Ants find their food by following chemical clues, so the caterpillars use a chemical disguise. Lipid chemicals in their skin mimic lipids in the plants they are feeding on. Hungry ants don't seem to realize that the caterpillars are there. They will even crawl over the caterpillars without attacking them.

49

MALAYSIAN SWALLOWTAIL CATERPILLAR

Papilio species

This swallowtail caterpillar seems to be staring at you, but its huge "eyes" are not real. They are only colored eyespots, and they are not even on its head. The caterpillar's real head is small and black and its real eyes are tiny. It can inflate its body to make the eyespots look even bigger, which makes the caterpillar look like a snake. That can be enough to scare away a hungry bird.

MADAGASCAR SILKMOTH

Borocera species

Moth caterpillars like these spin cocoons to protect themselves. Inside the cocoon they turn into a pupa, and later into an adult. People in Madagascar made "wild silk" from *Borocera* cocoons for centuries. They used the silk to make clothing and burial cloths. Today, villagers still weave this silk as a way to make extra money. Besides, they can also eat the pupae—a favorite food.

PUSS MOTH

Cerura vinula

If a Puss Moth caterpillar is threatened, it raises the front end of its body. It pulls in its head to reveal a pinkish "face" with black spots for "eyes." Then it lifts its two "tails" (modified prolegs), sticks a worm-like pink thread out of each one, and lashes them about. If that doesn't work, it can squirt painful acid from a gland under its head. Birds eat them anyway, but wasps and flies trying to lay eggs on the caterpillar's body may be warned off.

SILKMOTH CATERPILLAR FROM BRAZIL

Unknown species
Caterpillars have many enemies, so they need to protect themselves. Many moth caterpillars are armed with stinging hairs. The hairs are hollow, like hypodermic needles, and they can inject poison if they break off in your skin. Stinging caterpillars are often brightly colored. The colors are a warning to any enemy that comes near.

SILKMOTH CATERPILLAR FROM PERU

Unknown species
Many tropical silkmoth caterpillars
are covered with stinging hairs.
Some have stings that are itchy
and painful, but others are very
dangerous. The caterpillar of
Lonomia obliqua, a silkmoth
from southern Brazil, can kill you.
Hundreds of *Lonomia* caterpillars
may live in one fruit tree, so farmers
harvesting the fruit risk being stung
many times. About three people a
year die from *Lonomia* stings.

AUTOMERIS SILKMOTH

Automeris species

There are about 200 species of *Automeris* silkmoths, most of which live in tropical America. This photograph was taken in Peru. *Automeris* caterpillars are very colorful and they are known for their painful stings. One species, the Io Moth, lives in North America. Io Moth caterpillars are covered with bristles, and each bristle is connected to a poison gland. The bristles can break off in your skin, which releases their poison. The sting may only make you itch, but it can be very painful for some people.

FLANNEL MOTH CATERPILLAR

Family Megalopygidae

Disturb a flannel moth caterpillar and it will puff up into a cloud of furry hairs. Don't touch it! Hidden in its "fur" are sharp needles that may break off in your skin. When they do, they inject poisons that can cause terrible pain. Most flannel moths live in tropical America, but several very poisonous ones have reached the United States. Some tropical flannel moth caterpillars grow up to 3 inches (7.5 cm) long.

NEW GUINEA SLUG CATERPILLAR

Family Limacodidae

Slug caterpillars, like this one from New Guinea, are really weird. Their prolegs are hidden and tipped with suckers. Instead of crawling, they glide on their bellies, like garden slugs. Many are very colorful, and the colors warn you that they are armed. Slug caterpillars carry clusters of stinging hairs that can be very dangerous. The sting of the Saddleback Caterpillar, a slug caterpillar from North America, can make a person seriously ill.

TELEMACHUS MORPHO

Morpho telemachus
Morphos are beautiful butterflies from South America. Their caterpillars give off a smell like rotten tomatoes. If you touch one, it will rear up and flick its head from side to side. The caterpillar seems to be trying to stab you with its bristles. Don't worry—it's just an act! Its bristles seem to be harmless. Maybe it's trying to fool predators into thinking that it is a moth caterpillar with a dangerous sting.

COMMON TIT

Hypolycaena erylus teatus

The caterpillars of many hairstreaks, blues, and other small butterflies live with ants. Some cannot survive without them. Common Tits from tropical Asia lay their eggs in the nests of Weaver Ants. The ants take care of the caterpillars and protect them from enemies. In return, the caterpillars supply the ants with drops of sweet liquid. The caterpillars of some blues eat baby ants, but the ants they live with protect them anyway. This is because the caterpillars give off chemicals that keep the ants from attacking.

ORANGE-SPOTTED TIGER CLEARWING

Mechanitis polymnia
Most butterflies do not spin
cocoons. A butterfly pupa is called
a chrysalis—from the Greek word
for gold. The chrysalis of the
Orange-spotted Tiger Clearwing
does look like a little golden house.
These butterflies are being raised
on a farm in Colombia. Inside each
chrysalis, the caterpillar is slowly
turning into an adult.

MONARCH BUTTERFLY

Danaus plexippus
A Monarch butterfly egg takes four
days to hatch. As a caterpillar, it eats
milkweed leaves and grows for two
weeks. Then it spends 10 to 14 days
as a chrysalis before emerging as an
adult butterfly. After its wings dry, the
butterfly flies away—perhaps to join
the great Monarch migration. No one
butterfly lives to make the whole trip.
A Monarch flying north may be the
grandchild of a butterfly that flew
south the year before.

INDEX